THE
BIG
TIME

CARRIE
UNDERWOOD

VALERIE BODDEN

CREATIVE EDUCATION

CARRIE UNDERWOOD

TABLE OF CONTENTS

MEET CARRIE

Carrie stands on the stage. She sings the words, "Blown away." Behind her, a fake tornado swirls. It is filled with small pieces of paper. The paper spins around Carrie. It flies into the crowd as everyone cheers.

Carrie Underwood is a country music singer. She writes many of her own songs. Carrie's concerts are exciting to listen to and to watch. Many people think Carrie is the best female country singer today.

Carrie's singing won her three People's Choice Awards in 2009

CARRIE'S CHILDHOOD

Carrie was born March 10, 1983, in Muskogee, Oklahoma. She grew up in the nearby town of Checotah. Carrie lived with her parents and two older sisters. Carrie started singing in church when she was three.

Carrie with her mom in 2006

MUSKOGEE, OKLAHOMA

GETTING INTO MUSIC

G rowing up, Carrie listened to many kinds of music. She liked country music best. She learned how to play guitar and piano. When she was a teenager, she sang at festivals and talent shows. She sang in musical plays at school, too.

. . . .

The American Country Awards show gives a special guitar to winners

While she was at Oklahoma's North-eastern State University for college, Carrie sang in a country-western music show. But she did not plan to become a singer. She wanted to work in television news.

....

Carrie thought she would have to give up her dream of singing

THE BIG TIME

n 2005, Carrie took a year off college to be on the TV singing contest *American Idol*. On May 25, Carrie won the contest! She released her first **single** a month later. It was called "Inside Your Heaven."

After Carrie won American Idol, *her song sold nearly 1 million copies*

Some Hearts was Carrie's first album. People bought more than 7 million copies! Since 2006, Carrie was named Female **Vocalist** of the Year by the Academy of Country Music three times. Carrie has won six **Grammy Awards**. Her fourth album, Blown Away, came out in 2012.

Carrie won her third Grammy Award in 2008 for the song "Before He Cheats"

OFF THE STAGE

When she is not singing, Carrie spends time with her husband, hockey player Mike Fisher. Carrie and Mike have two dogs. Carrie and her husband are religious and go to church regularly.

....

Carrie and Mike got married in July 2010

WHAT IS NEXT?

In 2011, Carrie started acting. She starred in the movie *Soul Surfer*. She hopes to entertain people with her singing and acting for years to come!

After Soul Surfer *(left), Carrie continued winning awards for her music (right)*

WHAT CARRIE SAYS ABOUT ...

AMERICAN IDOL

"Millions of people all over the U.S. saw me do my best and my worst week to week on the show."

COUNTRY MUSIC

"To me, it's the most respectable kind of music. It's honest. The people are genuinely talented."

HER CHILDHOOD

"I was definitely a tomboy. I climbed trees, and I'd jump hay bales and play with the cows, and Dad would take me fishing."

GLOSSARY

Grammy Awards the most famous music awards in the United States

single one song sold by itself and not as part of an album with other songs

vocalist a singer

READ MORE

Newroad, Adele. *Carrie Underwood*. New York: Gareth Stevens, 2010.

Tieck, Sarah. *Carrie Underwood*. Minneapolis: Abdo, 2009.

WEBSITES

Carrie Underwood
www.carrieunderwoodofficial.com/us
This is Carrie's own website, with news and pictures.

Carrie Underwood Biography
http://www.people.com/people/carrie_underwood
This site has information about Carrie's life and many pictures, too.

INDEX

PUBLISHED BY Creative Education
P.O. Box 227, Mankato, Minnesota 56002
Creative Education is an imprint of The Creative Company
www.thecreativecompany.us

DESIGN AND PRODUCTION BY Christine Vanderbeek
ART DIRECTION BY Rita Marshall
PRINTED IN the United States of America

PHOTOGRAPHS BY Corbis (Phil Mucci/Retna Ltd., Lucy Nicholson), Getty Images (Jon Kopaloff/FilmMagic, Jason Merritt, Ethan Miller, Kevin Winter, Kevin Winter/AMA), iStockphoto (GYI NSEA, Pingebat, Cole Vineyard), Newscom (Will Binns/PacificCoastNews), Shutterstock (Helga Esteb, Featureflash, Mat Hayward, Jaguar PS, s_bukley)

LIBRARY OF CONGRESS CATALOGING-IN-PUBLICATION DATA
Bodden, Valerie.
Carrie Underwood / Valerie Bodden.
p. cm. — (The big time)
Includes index.
Summary: An elementary introduction to the life, work, and popularity of Carrie Underwood, an American country western singer known for her *American Idol* victory and such hit songs as "Inside Your Heaven."

ISBN 978-1-60818-476-7
1. Underwood, Carrie, 1983– —Juvenile literature. 2. Country musicians—United States—Biography—Juvenile literature.
I. Title.
ML3930.U53B63 2013
782.421642092—dc23 [B]   2013014552

9 8 7 6 5 4 3 2